playhouse

write

playhouse   playhouse   _____

eggin

write

eggin   eggin   _____

greenhouse

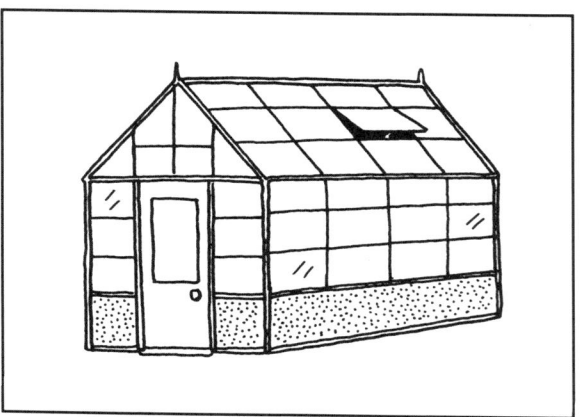

write

greenhouse   greenhouse   _____

playthings

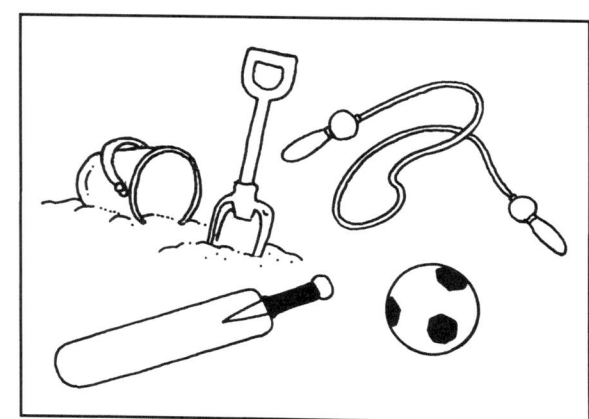

write

playthings   playthings   _____

asleep

write

asleep   asleep   _____

colour this

greenback

write

greenback greenback _____

outhouse

write

outhouse outhouse _____

buzzit

write

buzzit buzzit _____

write the words

 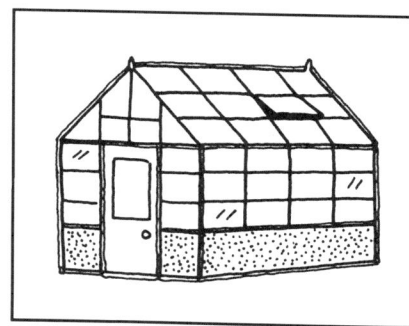 

colour the buzzit

these are black

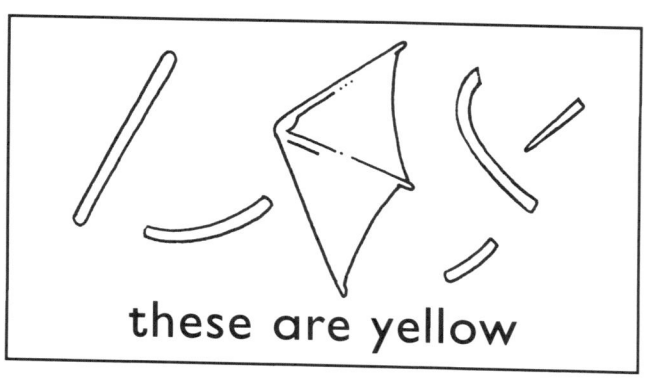
these are yellow

draw a greenhouse next to this tree

draw a big crack in the greenhouse

colour the crack black

write

this   is   a   greenhouse

_____

there   is   a   big   crack   in   it

_____

draw these things

playthings	eggin	greenhouse
buzzit	asleep	playhouse

draw an outhouse next to this house

draw a fuzzbuzz asleep on this mattress

colour the fuzzbuzz red and blue

colour the mattress yellow

colour the tin brown

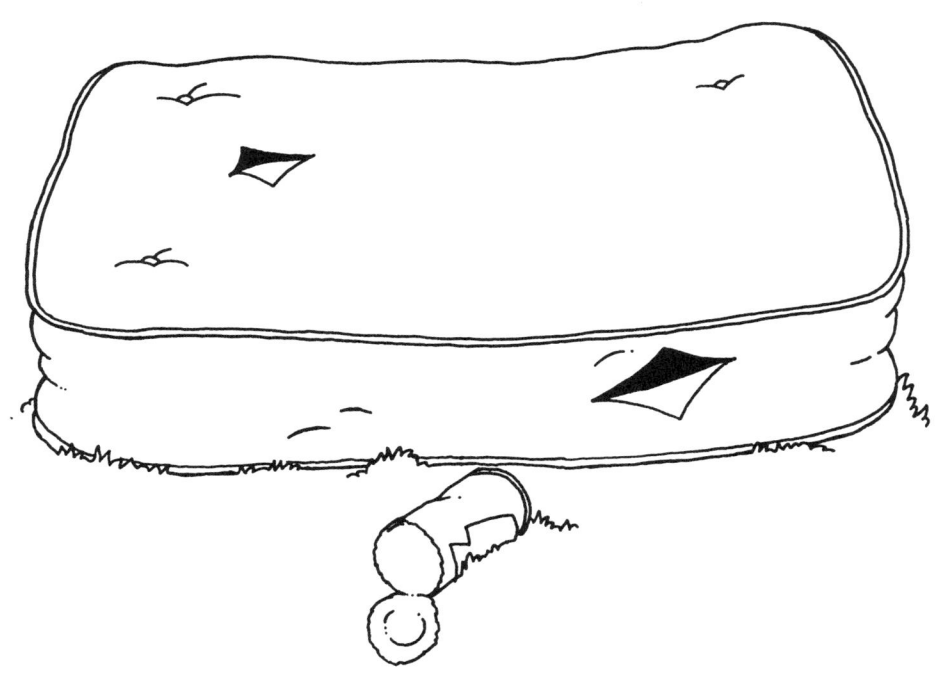

write

this   fuzzbuzz   is   asleep   on   the   mattress

can you read these words

some ink

an egg with a crack in it

a big tin

a van

an egg box

a spring

a black umbrella

a rock

an orange

a box

an apple

a ribbon

a tin can

a black tree

a letter

now write the words on the dump

the things from the dump

first read these words

this is red

these are green

this is orange

this is blue and red

this is black

this is orange and green

this is yellow

this is brown

this is black and yellow

next write them under these things

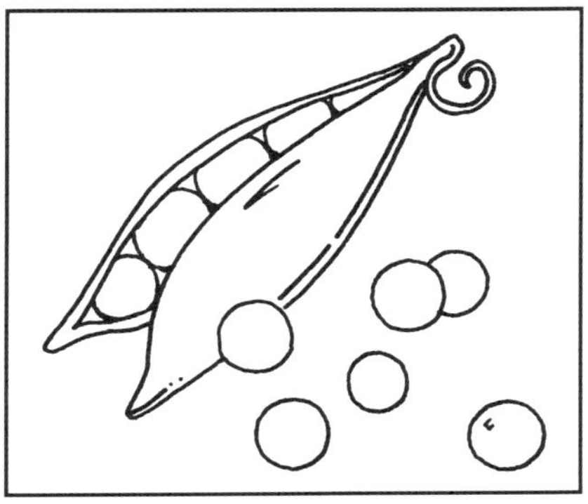

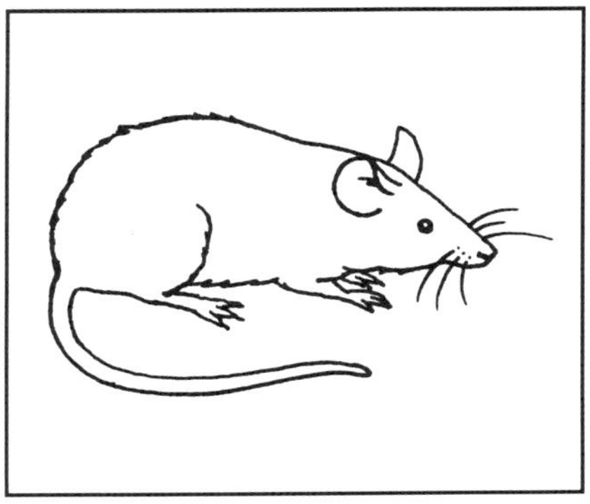

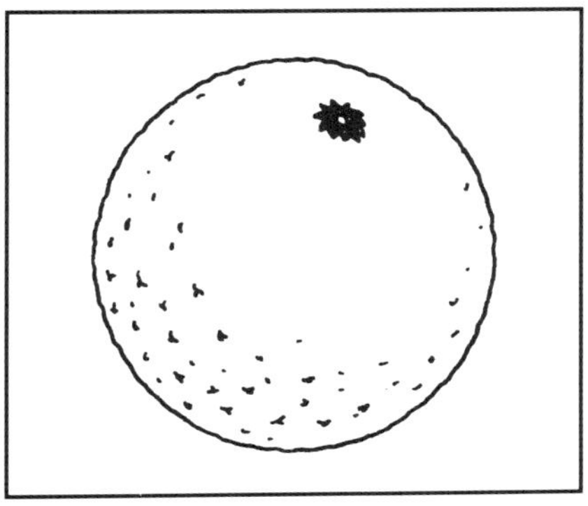

now colour them in

first read these words

        this jumps

        this is good fun

        you draw with this

        this drops from a tree

        you can see with these

        letters go in this

        this lives in a garden

        this is to sleep in

        you can read this

now write them under these things

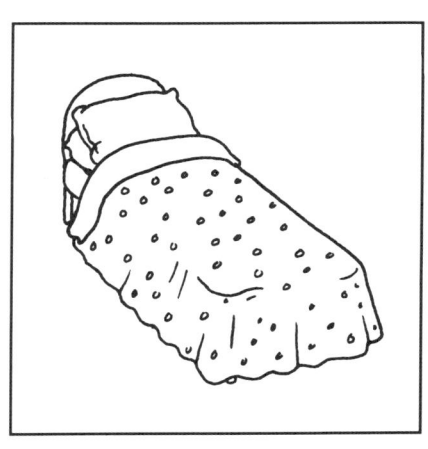

can you read these words

an umbrella

a greenhouse

some letters

an apple tree

an outhouse

the slinx

some apples

a mattress

an orange

a house

the buzzit

some playthings

eggin

a fuzzbuzz asleep on the mattress

a tin

a playhouse

now write them next to these things

colour this

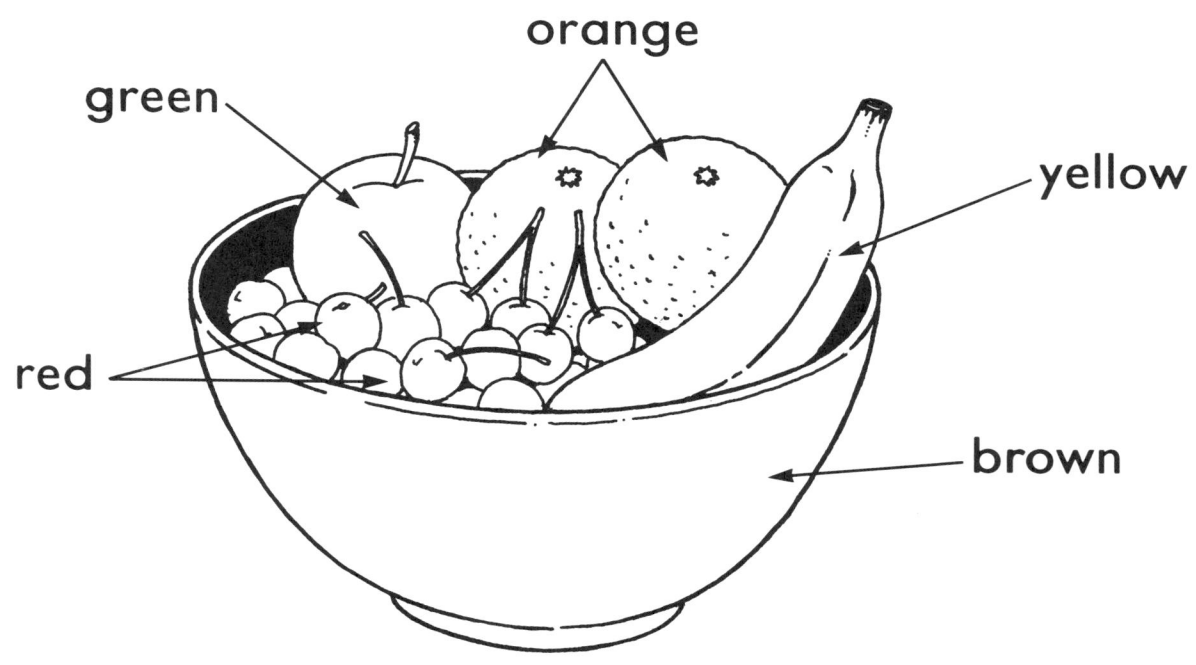

can you read these words

        he is asleep

        he is upset

        he is coming down

        he is mad

        he is going up

        he is happy

now write the words under these

this is a tree

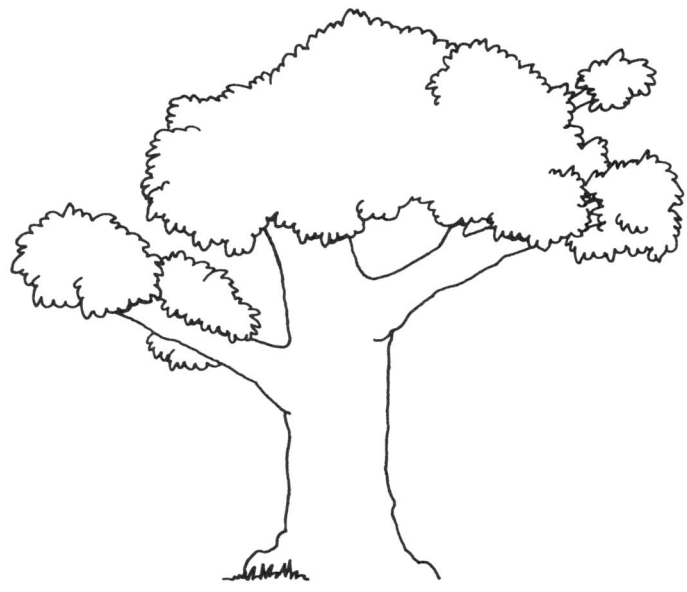

now draw these things

    a mattress under the tree

    some playthings on the mattress

    a big rock next to the mattress

    eggin up on the rock

    the slinx at the back of the tree

    a fuzzbuzz up in the tree

    the buzzit jumping down from the tree

first read **words 1** at the back
next you can read these

6.1   the big house

6.2   eggin and his playthings

6.3   the van

6.4   the buzzit

6.5   eggin and the fuzzbuzzes

6.6   the end of the buzzit

Write

Write

Write Write _____

Can you colour this?

Write

Can Can _____

Draw

Write
Draw Draw _____

Can you colour this?

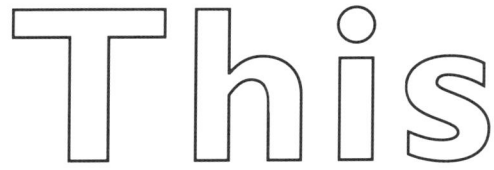

Write
This This _____

First

Write
First First _____

Can you colour this?

Write

He   He   _____

Ribbon

Write

Ribbon   Ribbon   _____

Can you colour this?

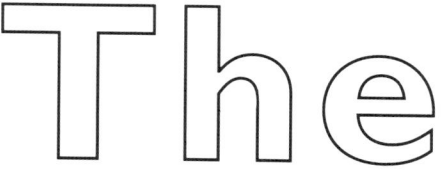

Write

The   The   _____

Creeps

Write

Creeps   Creeps   _____

Can you colour this?

Write

These   These   _____

Rock

Write

Rock   Rock   _____

In

Write

In   In   _____

Can you colour this?

Write

Now   Now   _____

Crack

Write

Crack   Crack   _____

Umbrella

Write

Umbrella   Umbrella   _____

Can you colour this?

Write

Some   Some   _____

Down

Write

Down   Down   _____

Can you colour this?

Write

They   They   _____

Write   Bump

Bump   Bump   _____

Can you colour this?

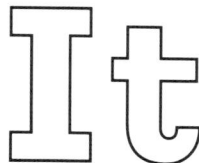

Write

It   It   _____

Blue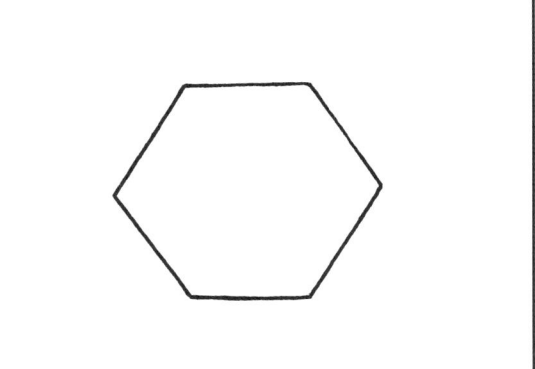

Write

Blue   Blue   _____

Can you colour this?

Write

There   There   _____

Next

Write

Next   Next   _____

Eggin

Write

Eggin　　Eggin　　_____

This is a garden.

Draw some playthings under the tree and next to the rock.

Draw a green box.
Next to the box, draw a yellow egg.

Can you go to the words?

these	Next
rock	These
it	It
next	Rock
umbrella	Creeps
write	Write
creeps	Umbrella
blue	The
some	Down
the	Blue
down	First
first	Some

(An arrow is drawn from "these" to "These".)

Draw these things.

Ribbon	Write	Crack
Blue	Next	Down
In	Eggin	Rock
Bump	First	Draw

Can you go to the words?

Eggin	there
There	he
Now	eggin
Crack	crack
He	now
Ribbon	bump
They	in
Bump	ribbon
In	can
Draw	they
This	this
Can	draw

Write the words.

_____   _____   _____

_____   _____   _____

_____   _____   _____

_____   _____   _____

Can you read these words?

      in   under   next to   on

Write them under these things.

Now write them in these.

Eggin is _____ the box.

The fuzzbuzz is _____ the umbrella.

The buzzit is _____ the tree.

The slinx is _____ the tin.

First, read these words.

The fuzzbuzz is out now.

Crack goes the egg.

This is a box.

He jumps out of the tree.

There is a fuzzbuzz in the egg.

The fuzzbuzz jumps out.

There is an egg under the box.

The fuzzbuzz gets into the tree.

Now write them under these.

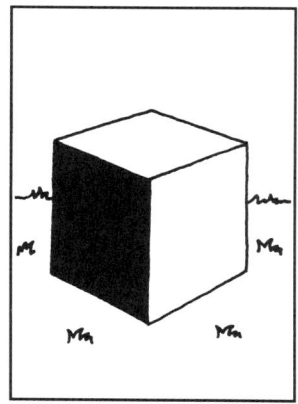

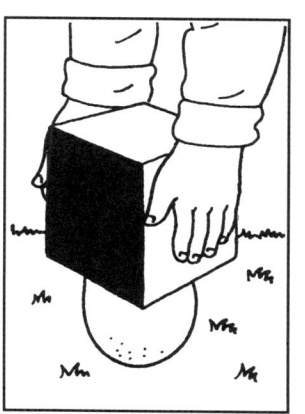

1

2

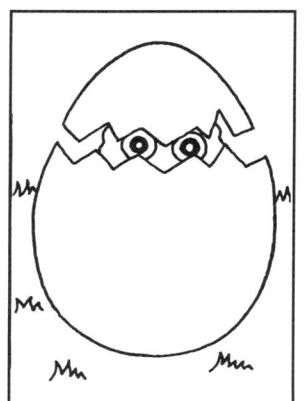

3 _____

4 _____

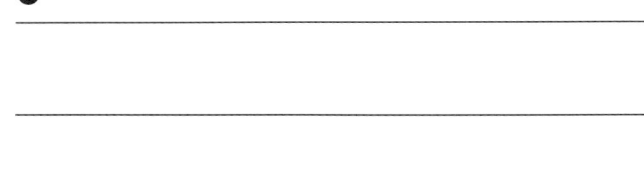

5 _____

6 _____

7 _____

8 _____

Can you read these words?

They buzz.

It drops in.

This goes to the dump.

He writes a letter.

It lives in a tree.

He can box.

This comes out of an egg.

This can rock.

These come up in spring.

Now write the words under these.

First, read these words.

> The slinx jumps out.
>
> They come out into the garden.
>
> Some of them play in the van.
>
> The fuzzbuzzes are upset.
>
> The fuzzbuzzes are in the house.
>
> They go to play on the mattress.
>
> Now they go to the dump.
>
> The slinx can see them.

Now write them under these.

1 _____

2 _____

3 _____

4 _____

5 _____

6 _____

7 _____

8 _____

Can you colour these black?

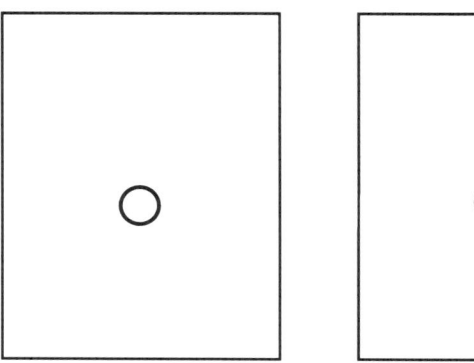 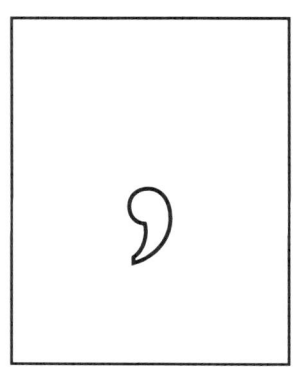  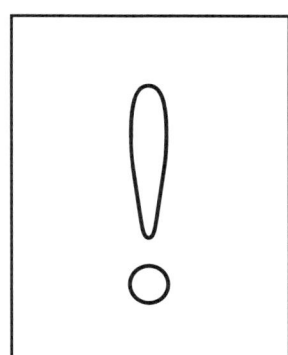

Can you see them in these and colour them red?

In the end, the slinx goes back.

The egg goes crack!

Can you see the slinx?

He is good.

Can you get it?

First, go and get the box.

Bump! The rock drops down.

Can you jump?

Down at the dump, the slinx is asleep.

Can you write these out?

an This is tree. apple

This is an apple tree.

apple down. The drops

picks up. it Eggin

puts in He box. a it

box The black. is

First, read these words.

The fuzzbuzzes go.

First, a spring goes into the tin.

Bump! The slinx comes down.

Crack! He goes into the rock.

The slinx gets into his tin.

Next, a rock goes onto the tree.

Can you see his bump?

He goes up and up.

Now write them under these.

1

2

3 _____

4 _____

5 _____

6 _____

7 _____

8 _____

First, read this.

> The first tin is blue.
>
> The next tin is yellow.
>
> The big tin is orange.
>
> The tin with the bump is red.
>
> The tin on the box is brown.
>
> The box is black.
>
> The tin at the end is green.

Now colour them in.

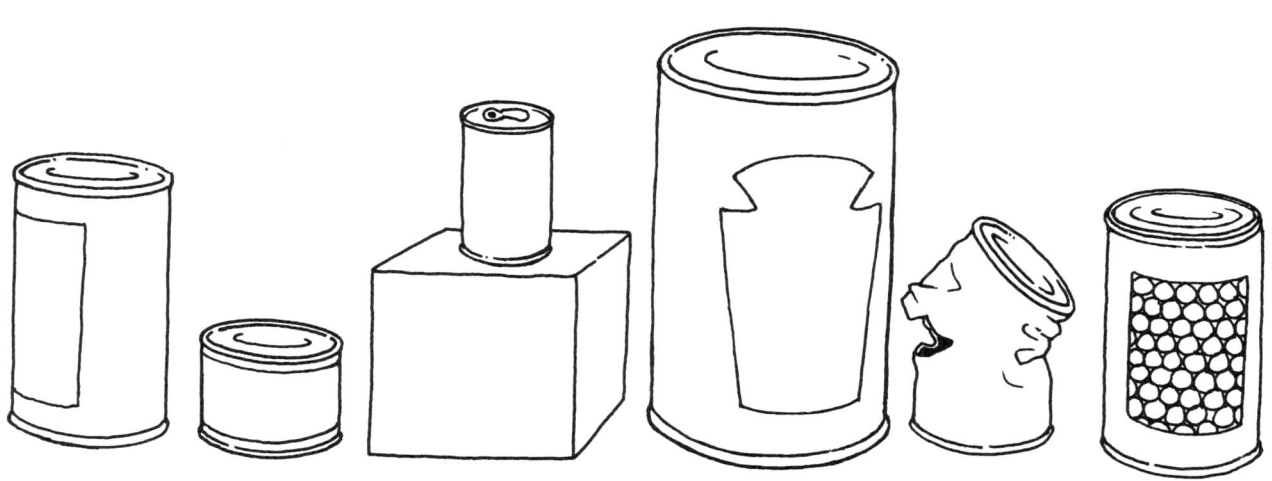

First, read **words 2** at the back.
Next, you can read these.

6.7   Eggin the good

6.8   Umbrella Rock

6.9   The Creeps

6.10   Eggin comes back

6.11   The Blue Ribbon

6.12   Down with the Creeps

words 1

buzzit ☐   outhouse ☐   greenback ☐

playhouse ☐   eggin ☐   asleep ☐

greenhouse ☐   playthings ☐

words 2

Next ☐   Eggin ☐   There ☐   Blue ☐

Crack ☐   Now ☐   In ☐   Rock ☐

These ☐   Creeps ☐   It ☐   Bump ☐

They ☐   Down ☐   Some ☐   Umbrella ☐

Ribbon ☐   The ☐   He ☐   First ☐

This ☐   Draw ☐   Can ☐   Write ☐

Oxford University Press